APPLE TREE

APPLE TREE

WRITTEN AND ILLUSTRATED BY PETER PARNALL

Macmillan Publishing Company   New York
Collier Macmillan Publishers   London

Macmillan Publishing Company, 866 Third Avenue, New York, NY 10022. Collier Macmillan Canada, Inc.
Printed in the United States of America. First Edition.   10   9   8   7   6   5   4   3   2   1
The text of this book is set in 14 point Baskerville. The illustrations are rendered in pencil and watercolor.
Library of Congress Cataloging-in-Publication Data   •   Parnall, Peter. Apple Tree.
Summary: Describes the many ways an apple tree interacts with insects, birds, and other animals during a full
year of its development. 1. Apple—Ecology—Juvenile literature. 2. Animal ecology—Juvenile literature.
3. Seasons—Juvenile literature. [1. Apple—Ecology. 2. Animal ecology. 3. Ecology] I. Title.
QH541.14.P37   1987   583'.372   86-23730   ISBN 0-02-770160-3

To Byrd,
who helps us see

It is thick and gnarled. Some branches seem like witch's claws, poking, grasping, twisted like a mass of melted wire. It is a world for insects, birds, mammals, lichens, moss, and me. My apple tree. There were others, too, planted years ago by an early German settler, but they are gone. I don't know why. Just rotten stumps remain, looking like skeletons against the sky. Maybe bugs killed them. Maybe the cold finally got into their bones, or maybe they died just from being old. This one lives on, hollow but strong, and says, "We were here."

"We were here."

After cold April rains fill every crevice in the tree, making pools in holes where branches used to grow, mosquitoes lay their eggs. Now, as pink buds strain to spread a wide quilt of flowers over the gray, brittle branches, the larvae twist and dive in anticipation of flight soon to come.

I see Bumblebee dart and hover, swoop and drone, hardly missing a single flower, gathering what pollen Honeybee has left behind. Many different-sized flies pretend they are bees, all striped and dangerous looking to a hungry bird. Three types of ants and bugs of all kinds hurry to gather all they can before warmer days force wilted blossoms to the ground.

When the flowers are gone, green leaves soften the lines of tangled branches. Lichens in patches color the bark, and moss grows on the wetter part the sun rarely sees—the northwest side. There chickadees flutter from a nesting hole, cleaning damp, grassy litter from last year's nest and returning with fresher morsels of grass and moss on which to lay their speckled white eggs. The hole seems so small.

How do they fit?

In early summer I find Robin building a perfect round nest
near where I used to sit and pretend I was flying a glider
with passengers like Ghengis Khan and Alexander the
Great. The flights will have to be postponed until the bright
blue eggs hatch and the babies fly into the world beyond
the tree. During the days Robin flies and weaves and fusses,
and once her eggs are laid she watches. And watches …
beetles.

A great horde of beetles! They stay about a week. Thousands of skinny green beetles I am sure are going to eat the tree to shreds, lurch around, under, over, and alongside each other, ignoring any passerby, and they don't eat a thing! Just fuss and lurch. I try to look them up in a book and can't find a "lurch" beetle. But that's what they are. By now yellow jackets are examining young apples, wondering how soon they can make their caves and tunnels; and Woodpecker visits each day, remembering the storehouse of winter treats he found months ago beneath the peeling, gray, crusty bark.

Nuthatch, too. He comes here darting upside down or headside up, searching for eggs of bugs hidden in bark splits or the thousands of holes Woodpecker has made. Some bugs race for cover among the lichens, or in the hundreds of crannies in the bark. Others choose mossy places to hide, where Nuthatch doesn't like to walk. At least I've never seen him do it. What I have seen him do is grab a little worm and stuff it tightly into a crevice, saving it for later.

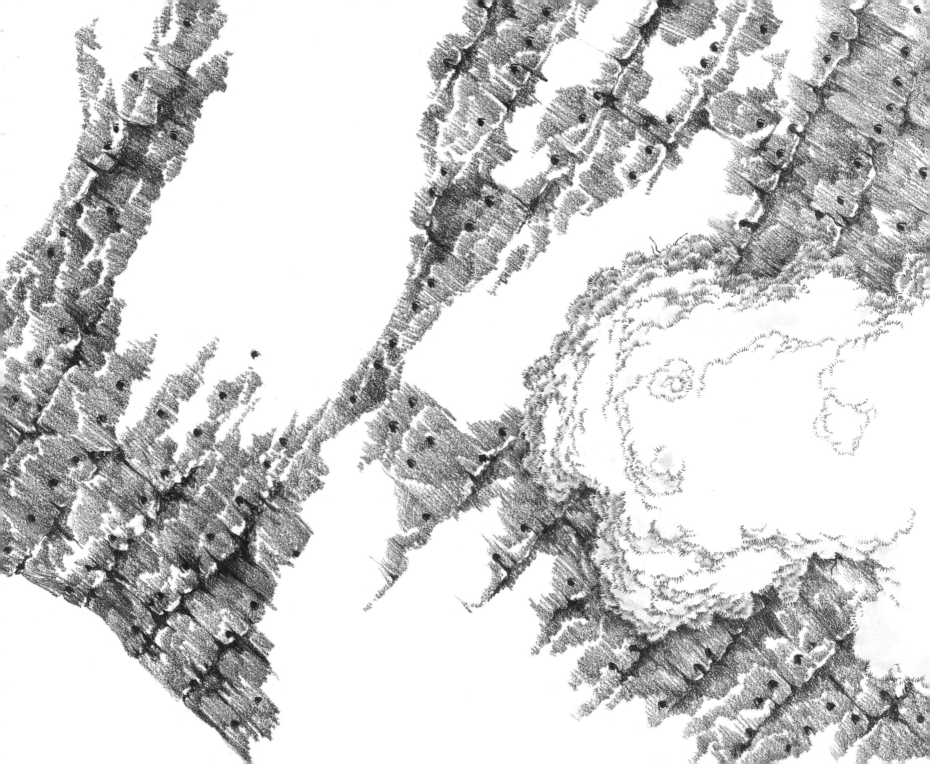

Late in the summer, long after the robins fly, I am high on their branch looking at the nest and wondering how they managed to get it so round. Tightly woven grasses, all uniform in size, are mixed with mud and form a nest so round it seems it might have been molded on a ball of some kind. Or a coconut. I stare into the perfect little nest, and a tiny blue egg chip reminds me of who has been there. Suddenly there is a movement below! Down past my feet. Down on the ground. Fuzzy antlers sway, and I hold my breath as Deer wishes for fallen apples to appear.

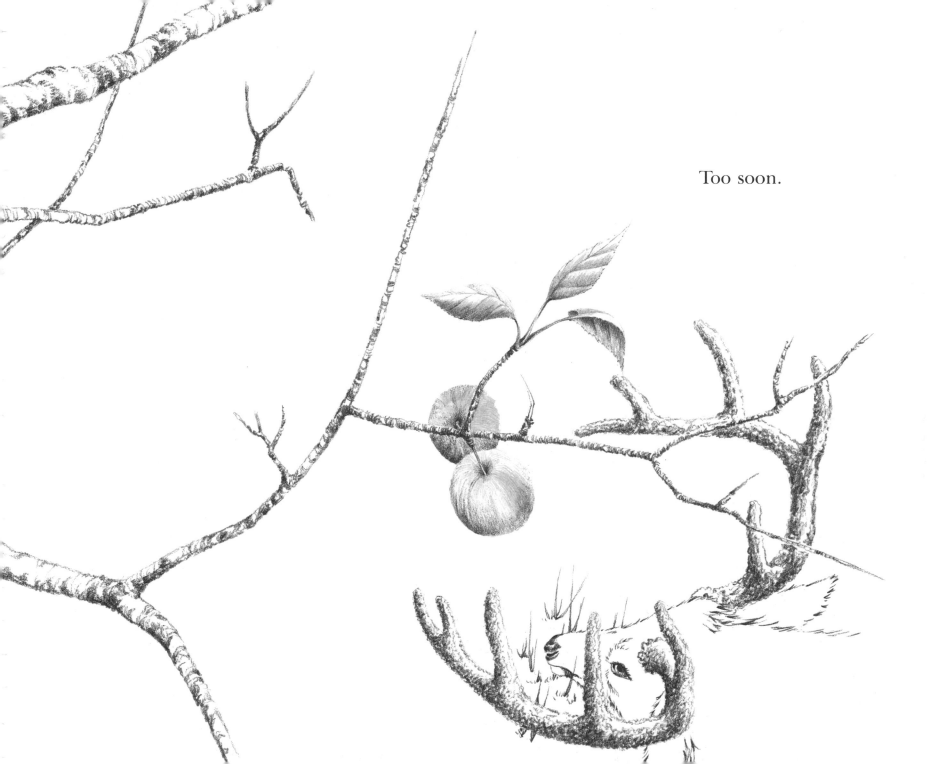

Too soon.

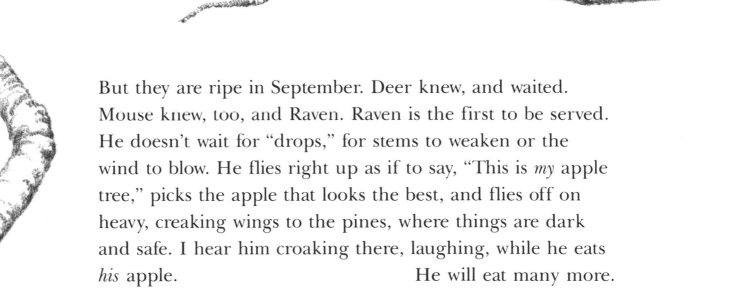

But they are ripe in September. Deer knew, and waited.
Mouse knew, too, and Raven. Raven is the first to be served.
He doesn't wait for "drops," for stems to weaken or the
wind to blow. He flies right up as if to say, "This is *my* apple
tree," picks the apple that looks the best, and flies off on
heavy, creaking wings to the pines, where things are dark
and safe. I hear him croaking there, laughing, while he eats
his apple.   He will eat many more.

Crisp fall air turns leaves to yellow, and they begin to rattle in the breeze. Rarely is an insect seen abroad, risking its life in the chilly air or exposing itself as prey for birds building up their bodies for winter or a long flight south. The apples are dropping now, giving ants and wasps a last sweet taste of fall and providing a storehouse of food for Mouse to hoard in his larder beyond the lawn. His paths begin to form, and when snow falls they will be tunnels—tunnels to his home, keeping him safe from winter claws and prying eyes.

Old Coon fusses deep within the hollow trunk, testing, patting, curling about, and making do with what soft, rotten wood is there to form a cozy winter lair. She is fat from our corn, apples, and sweet horse feed and will be snug down there when thirty-below winds tear at the fingertips of our old brittle tree.

Snow finally comes, burying apples and grass deep beneath its cloak, covering branches, holes, lichens. Even the tiniest bud that never grew has its little cap of snow. What apples remain tight to their stems are brown now, bobbing, swaying in the wind, beckoning to Pine Grosbeak and Blue Jay to leave the forest and have a last sweet taste of fall before the fruit is frozen too hard to eat. At dawn Deer is there below the tree, pawing great slashes in the snow and nibbling at the few apples still frozen to the ground.

Mouse is, too.

It's deep winter now. The sun rises, painting
snow-covered branches a brilliant pink, and the
gold-brown apples turn to an orange glow.

Deer comes no more. He stays deep in the forest,
eating buds and barks and pawing up moss and acorns
from beneath the snow. Coon sleeps deep, but Grosbeak
and Jay keep coming to the few high apples, hammering at
the frozen pulp made sweeter by temperatures too low to
permit life for fall creatures, creatures who now huddle
in crevices or sleep the winter away.

The tree stands quiet under its blanket of snow. Sometimes
all that shows are the shoots that grew last spring, shoots
that grew straight up ... skyward, toward the place where
the old, battered tree wants to grow.

I wonder how it can stand the cold.

Because it knows.   It knows Robin will come home.

PETER PARNALL has illustrated over seventy books, three of which have been named Caldecott Honor Books. Several of his books have been on the *New York Times* "Best Illustrated Books of the Year" list, and he has won awards from the Society of Illustrators and the American Institute of Graphic Arts. He has had artwork exhibited in major fine-art museums and has had over two dozen one-man shows.

Mr. Parnall's special interests include horses, sailing, competitive shooting, and woodland management. He lives on a farm on the coast of Maine, where he raises wood and sheep.